DON'T FEED THE TROLL

BUILDING A HEALTHY WRITING CAREER

J.S. DIXON

NANETTE M. DAY

BUILDING A HEALTHY WRITING CAREER SERIES

Series link- https://www.amazon.com/J-S-Dixon/e/B07YGXWP1K/

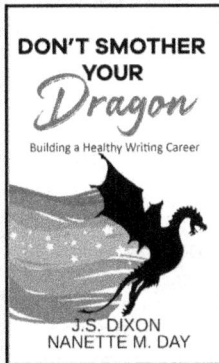

Don't Smother Your Dragon: Building a Healthy Writing Career

Your dragon will fly fast and fly confidently

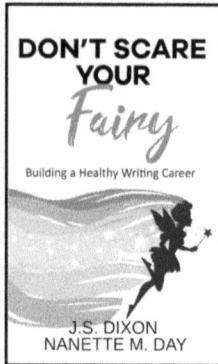

DON'T SCARE YOUR *Fairy*
Building a Healthy Writing Career
J.S. DIXON
NANETTE M. DAY

Don't Scare Your Fairy: Building a Healthy Writing Career

Keep your fairy happy and flappy!

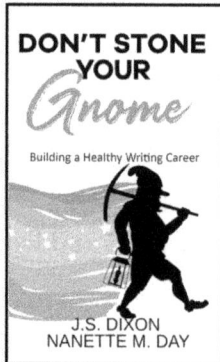

DON'T STONE YOUR *Gnome*
Building a Healthy Writing Career
J.S. DIXON
NANETTE M. DAY

Don't Stone Your Gnome: Building a Healthy Writing Career

Protect your gnome—after all, it's your name on the line.

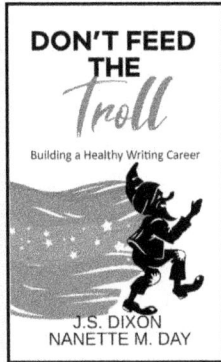

DON'T FEED THE *Troll*

Building a Healthy Writing Career

J.S. DIXON
NANETTE M. DAY

Don't Feed the Troll: Building a Healthy Writing Career

Keep those trolls where they belong: under the bridge!

FOREWORD

The Building a Healthy Writing Career series helps you succeed as a writer by nourishing your muse, heeding your inner voice, doing the work consistently, and eliminating time/energy drains from your workday. The individual books can be read in any order and include appendixes with additional resources.

INTRODUCTION

Welcome to *Don't Feed the Troll: Building a Healthy Writing Career*. We're glad to have you along for this wonderful journey into your writing career.

You're probably wondering how a troll can affect your writing? The truth is that trolls can affect us in so many ways that we don't even realize, but we'll get to that soon enough. First, we want to give you an idea of what you'll find in this book.

This book isn't fluff. If you want fluff, Jules is offering snugglefests with her two long-haired cats. They have the fluff, although they aren't always up for snuggles. This series is information for writers who want to be informed, stay informed, and get more done. It's a B.S.-free zone. We share the truth, and we keep it real, as the truth isn't always pretty.

We won't sugarcoat what you need to do and what

can go wrong. We, Jules and Nanette, are happy people. Butterflies and rainbows shoot from our lips on a daily basis. Yeah, maybe not quite that happy. The normal amount of happy, plus a dash. We know that not everything's going to be butterflies and rainbows all the time, but we do our best to stay focused on the end goal: producing good writing consistently.

This book isn't gospel. We aren't preaching to you that this is the only way to succeed as a writer. Rather, we noticed that many writers in our support groups were facing the same challenges as we were, and we decided to share the methods, techniques, and insights that have worked for us to keep us on track.

We know you are the president of your business, but the reading population can make or break your authorship. And it is a ship. It's floating in rough and calm waters. It's vulnerable to infiltration and misdirection. You don't want to run aground or hit that proverbial iceberg. By following a few simple tips and hints, you can avoid crashing and keep smooth sailing.

So that's what this book isn't. But there are a million things this book is. We won't bore you with 999,997 of them because you're going to find out, but the top three that we want you to know about are: experience, candid delivery, and take-it-or-leave-it advice.

Cumulatively, Jules and Nanette have two decades of writing experience, and we've written more than 60 published works of all sizes, from micro-fiction to 100K+-word novels in a variety of genres, from LGBT romance to sweet holiday stories to grit lit stories that would make even the most fiendish of trolls run and hide.

We know how hard writing is and that the industry changes constantly. What we're giving you is our knowledge and what we've researched from other authors who have also been there and done that. We've faced everything you're probably going through. We love writing and we want to help you love it, love it again, or love it even more, depending on where you are in your writing life cycle.

This book contains candid delivery with a little humor. We play up the "troll" angle to help you understand just how devasting lost productivity can be to your writing career. We also include Action Steps that will help you learn to recognize troll-like behavior, take steps to minimize the harm trolls can inflict, and approach your writing career with a focus on maximizing productivity while still embracing the creative freedom that first attracted you to writing. Jules isn't a fan of sugar coating anything except for the rim of her sweettart martini, and Nanette lives in the middle of the country where she makes cows cry, so we're going to be honest and persuasive. That's a promise.

Ultimately, this is your career. We understand that. You get to decide what you will and won't take from this. We can guide you, but the writer is the one who determines their success. If you decide to disregard the advice and information we provide, all we would ask is that you let us know what you did differently and how it worked. Writing can be a solitary endeavor, but we're here for you and we won't judge. We've developed a Facebook community and we welcome you to join us; even if you just lurk, you're welcome.

Okay, it's time. Are you ready to take on that troll that's been sapping your productivity? Let's get to it!

1- THE AGE OF THE TROLL (YUCK!)

The word *troll* is used in a variety of ways in today's world. For the purposes of this book, we define a troll as any person or activity that takes us away from what we want and/or should be doing and detracts from our efforts to make a living by writing. Basically, a troll is a time and energy suck that drains us of the ability to complete our writing tasks.

Some trolls are quite easy to pick out, like the person who leaves a nasty review without (by their own admission) ever reading our work. After reading the review we might get angry and indignant, telling all our friends and fans about what a jerk this person is. Meanwhile, inside we might be questioning if the troll has somehow seen the truth when no one else has and then called us out for being the fraud we are (this self-doubt is known as imposter syndrome, which we will explore more in the chapter The Troll in the Mirror).

A key point to note, and one we will come back to again and again, is that we allowed this troll's single activity to affect us. We stopped writing so we could share our anger, whether by calling a friend or posting on social media. A social media post will continue to show up in our feeds, being bumped up each time people comment and react to it. As a result, we will relive that anger over and over, each time needing to detox before we can focus on our writing. Well played, troll.

Yes, you read that right. Nanette complimented the troll (just to clarify: Jules does not believe in complimenting trolls, although she does recognize the power they can hold over us). The fact is, trolls are good at what they do, which is what makes them so dangerous for us. As the previous example shows, a few clicks of the keyboard, which probably took the troll all of thirty seconds to complete, has us running around, not writing, for several minutes, hours, even days! As a writer, wouldn't you love it if, for every hour of writing you completed, your readers spent hours, days, and even months reacting to your writing, talking about it, and sharing it with their friends and family? So yes, (small) props to trolls for being effective at what they do.

Ultimately, we allow trolls to affect us in a negative way. This book and the ideas we discuss in it provide tools for helping you stop trolls in their tracks. Just remember that the only person you can control is yourself (and to some extent your characters if you write fiction, although Nanette would argue that we don't control our characters either). So this book focuses predominantly on what we can do to protect ourselves from trolls. We will note when to involve others, when appropriate (such as social media owners or the police). Please note that it is our deepest, sincerest wish that no reader ever has to work with the police to deal with a troll. We just don't want anyone to ever have to experience that level of trolldom.

Before we discuss ways to protect yourself, we have to talk about the different kinds of trolls so you can understand which tools work best. We also want to help you get better at identifying trolls because they really are sneaky little buggers that seem to create an infestation right when we're in the zone in our writing. To help with identifying trolls, we are going to share various examples of both online and offline troll behavior. First, though, we want you to start getting into the troll-free mindset. Take a look at Action Step #1 so you can finetune your troll-identifying goggles.

Action Step #1

For the next few days, every time you stop writing, make a note of why you are stopping and how long your break will be. Are you stopping to walk the dog, do some marketing, or check your email? All are perfectly legitimate activities. Before you actually start these non-writing activities, predict how long you be away from writing. Make a note of that time. When you return to your writing, how close were you to your predicted time? What caused you to spend more (or less) time away from writing? Keep collecting this information as we discuss the different types of trolls.

2-THE ALL-TOO-FAMILIAR TROLL

For most people, the word *troll* evokes an image or feeling about a specific type of behavior: bullying—often anonymous bullying. This is what we call the All-Too-Familiar-Troll.

We've all seen examples of this kind of troll behavior. Elise Moreau explains that, "in simple terms, trolling is when someone comments or responds to something you post [on social media], usually in a confrontational way that is designed to garner a strong, emotional reaction." Such troll behavior can be characterized as being deliberate, (usually) random, unsolicited, and almost always public. The goal is to evoke a reaction.

Why do they troll? Who knows! There are many theories floating around. Some say the anonymity of our increasingly online world makes it easier for people to be ugly. There is likely some truth in this, but that doesn't explain troll behaviors from known sources, which we will discuss in the next chapter. Other people have claimed that trolls are lonely, angry, sad, narcissistic, and/or attention seekers who genuinely do not see their behavior as being trollish. Again, there may be some truth to this, but it is definitely not true for all trolls everywhere, as the many troll farms that have emerged prove.

Troll farms. Ugh. Yes, we now have to deal with an entire industry that has sprung up to promote troll behaviors. Troll farms are where people are organized into groups or teams whose sole purpose is to comment on blogs, forums, and social media to perpetuate disinformation. So far, such troll farms seem to be targeting predominantly political issues, but any time a person calls upon their fans and followers to attack another person, they are essentially coordinating an impromptu troll farm. Readers can also self-organize into troll farms, basically jumping on the bandwagon to attack a writer.

A relatively recent example of this was the #Cocky-Gate drama inspired by a romance writer who attempted to trademark the word "cocky" and all its derivatives. (We're giving you enough information to Google this issue if you want to learn more, but we really don't condone such behavior so we don't want to promote that author.) When the author sent cease and desist letters to other authors who used the word in their titles, those authors made this information public, and their fans flooded the trademark-seeker's Amazon pages with 1-star reviews (which have since mysteriously disappeared ... hmm).

As writers, we encounter these kinds of trolls in various contexts. Probably the most common occurrence is when readers leave bogus reviews. Reviews can be bogus for several reasons, but the most common troll comments or reviews occur when a reader doesn't even read the book or article before leaving a review/comment. Instead, they might be reacting to the title/headline or topic. Have you ever read a review where the reviewer says "I didn't read this book" or "I only read the free preview" and then goes on to offer their (usually very low-star) review? This is often trollish behavior because the reviewer wants to comment on something specific that may or may not have to do with the writing. This is especially common when the topic of the writing is considered a lightning rod issue; current examples include the vaccine/anti-vaccine debate, the #MeToo movement, and anything political.

Goodreads is notorious for trolls. As Jules often says, Goodreads likes the drama. And why wouldn't it? Drama means more eyes on its site, and more traffic leads to more revenues in some fashion. Goodreads, owned by Amazon, has become notorious for truly nasty reviews. Nanette actually had a trollish entity visit one of her pen names, leaving the following one-star review for a collection of short stories in which the characters "face down their darkest monsters" (per the blurb):

> I don't like short stories anyway, but these were really depressing. You have to wonder about someone who would write a whole book of stories with such horrible terrible people.

Okay, so this is not the biggest troll we've seen, but let's break this down a bit. First, the reviewer doesn't like short stories, but chooses to comment on a collection of short stories. Well, maybe something about the book's blurb worked and intrigued the reader to try reading something new. Yay! But then the reviewer questions the type of person the writer is, which has absolutely nothing to do with the writing itself. It's not a stretch to conclude that this reviewer is suggesting that Nanette is a horrible, terrible person. (Nanette here: I just have to say that I laughed at this review because the stories in the collection reviewed included characters that were far, far, FAR from the most depraved characters I have ever written.)

Of course, if you start reading a book or article and cannot finish it for a specific reason, that is a legitimate issue to note in a review. You might find the author's writing style off-putting or the storyline boring, which you can note in your comments. As authors, we have to remember that reviews are for other readers, not the authors.

This kind of troll behavior—commenting on something the reviewer hasn't read—isn't reserved for just reviews. Think about how often you see posts on social media that share an article or book, and someone who has so obviously not read the shared info leaves a comment. One particularly funny example follows:

Even if you didn't catch the "dyes" in the headline, the first line of the article makes it clear that Ms. White has comedic chops in writing as well (spoiler alert: she's not a natural blonde). The commenter didn't read the title carefully and didn't open the article to get clarification.

Of course, this example probably is not truly troll

behavior, but rather an honest mistake. Yet it can quickly turn into a troll-like situation without warning.

Let's pretend you shared this post on your author social media account because you and your fans enjoy a good play on words. The mistaken contributor makes a comment, and then others comment on his comment, using all sorts of adjectives that are less than flattering. Now you are faced with dealing with this situation. You have to take time and energy from your writing to diffuse the situation and save a fan (or more).

In addition, a troll could comment on the post itself. They might launch into a diatribe about how comedy today is so much worse than it used to be and people should go back to Vaudeville. The troll would likely point out specific (popular) comedians of our day (perhaps even the venerable Ms. White herself) and call them all sorts of hacks, wannabes, or humorless. In the process, the troll would insult a good chunk of your fan base by concluding that anyone who enjoys such types of simplistic comedy must be less than intelligent. (Nanette here: I just want to clarify that plays on words and puns are sophisticated forms of humor; both Jules and I understand this and appreciate a good pun.)

We'll discuss ways to deal with the All-Too-Familiar Trolls in Chapter 6 Troll-Proofing Your

Writing Sanctuary, but if you just can't wait to find out, the answer is simple: Ignore them.

I know, I know, that's not what you want to read. You want to learn about ways to eradicate them from the online space. But the thing about All-Too-Familiar Trolls is that even if you could eradicate them (and spoiler: you can't), fifty more immediately show up to take their place. They are like the mythological Hydra on steroids. Leave the slaying of the trolls to your heroes and heroines. Your job as a writer is to ignore, ignore, ignore.

Action Step #2

Tracking troll activity might sound counter-intuitive (considering we just said to ignore them), but this is a stepping-stone to help recognize when troll activity is happening, because not all trolls are as obvious as the All-Too-Familiar Troll. Create a tracking sheet with the following columns: Troll, Activity, Where, Your Reaction (time spent). We're going to use this tracking sheet for the next couple of chapters as well, so make sure you have plenty of room to track troll activity. Any time you encounter a troll online, whether on your social media, articles, or reviews or someone else's, make a note of what kind of troll you saw (we'll discuss more types in the following chapters), why their activity was trollish, where you spotted the troll, and what your reaction was (ignore, ignore, ignore for the All-Too-Familiar Trolls), including how much time (if any) you spent reacting.

Remember that your reaction should include any time that distracts you from work, so if you see some trolls on a colleague's social media and you have an emotional reaction to them, which you then discuss with others, all of that time should be included on your tracking sheet.

3-TROLLS ON THE FRIENDS AND FAMILY PLAN

When we define trolls as anyone who is sucking our time and energy away from writing, we have to realize that friends, colleagues, and family members can also be trolls. Now, we all have obligations to our friends and family, and we are not referring to the time and energy spent on those. When your cat demands to be fed, he is not being a troll (if he sprawls over your keyboard while you're typing, that's a different story ... kidding!). The need to take care of friends and family and nurture those relationships do not fall within the realm of trolldom.

But ...

Yes, there's always a but.

Just so we're all on the same page, we're going to outline a few assumptions. We assume that readers of this book are creative types in the publishing industry (or a similar type of area). We're going to assume that you don't produce your content while sitting in an office owned by your employer. If you do, no problem. You'll still benefit from the discussion that follows. We're going to guess that most of you have a home office that could be as little as some counterspace in the kitchen, or you write in the local coffee shop during your breaks. If you're lucky, you have a dedicated home office with a closing door and defined "office hours" when you write.

Based on these assumptions, we're going to discuss some other types of trolls that you might not realize are sucking your time and energy from writing. We'll start with the professional colleagues first.

The Pro Trolls

The pro trolls are not members of some certified trolldom. They are simply your fellow writers and other colleagues in the publishing industry, including publishers, graphic artists, editors, mentors, models, and event organizers (to name a few). These people are supposed to be your support group. They are supposed to help you learn as a creator, grow your skills, push yourself to meet new challenges head on, and accomplish more than you ever thought possible.

Unfortunately, they can also demonstrate trollish behavior that can actually force you to detour from your well-laid plans for achieving success. Let's look at some examples.

Google It Troll

If you're like many creatives, you probably are part of a professional association of some sort. You might be a member of Facebook groups or receive messages on a listserv discussion group. You might have a critique group that meets online. Basically, any time people get together, in person or online, the chances are you will encounter the Google It Troll.

The Google It Troll seems harmless enough, but it's the one that makes Nanette pull all her hair out. Repeatedly. It's not a good look. This troll will ask what seems to be a fairly innocuous question, and others in the group will quickly jump in to answer, wanting to provide a supportive and helpful group for all members. An example is "How do I upload my ebook to an online platform?" If you saw such a question, you would assume the person is a newbie and you might feel compelled to help because you are a good human being.

However, the troll continues to post similar questions. They might ask how to find a good cover designer, where to submit a short story, what is the difference between passive and active voice, or (Nanette's favorite) what do to about a bad review. Again, you want to be helpful with anyone seeking insights, but really what this person is doing is expecting others to do the research for them. If you instinctively search for an answer on Google (or your web search tool of choice), then why doesn't the person asking the question do the same? Because somewhere deep down, and probably without even realizing it, they want someone else to do the work for them. They want someone else to read all the information, analyze it, then parse it into bite-sized chunks that are easy to understand.

Congratulations, you have become an unpaid research assistant instead of writing your own stories.

The issue is compounded when the questions are being posted in a forum where others have asked (and answered) the same questions. In other words, the troll apparently didn't bother to search/read past posts and feedback.

Just to clarify, not everyone who posts a question is a Google It Troll, and you should absolutely answer questions when you feel you have something worthwhile to share. But be aware that this kind of troll behavior can be reinforced by immediately providing answers. One tactic that both Jules and Nanette have adopted when answering questions for possible Google It Trolls is to start our answers with "when I Googled your question" (or some variation). Basically, you are reminding the question-asker to do the work before asking questions.

Whether you respond to the Google It Troll or not is up to you. Just remember that taking time away from your work to do unpaid research work for another author is not always the best use of your time.

The Drama Queen Troll

Who doesn't love a good drama? Actually, a lot of people, but that's a discussion for another time. There are some people who thrive on drama, and not always in a healthy way. Then there are the trolls who feel so alive when drama enters their lives that they absolutely must share it with everyone they know. Let us introduce you to the Drama Queen Troll.

There are so many examples of drama-lovers in the troll community that it's hard to know where to start. One issue that we see repeatedly is an author going all crazy on social media because they just discovered that their book was pirated and they are determined to single-handedly bring down the Great Pirate Empire (as soon as they ask others how to do so).

Okay, just so we're all clear: Piracy is bad. Piracy is the bunion on the stinkiest foot of the ugliest troll who hasn't showered in centuries or even millennia. And anyone who can bring down the Great Pirate Empire permanently will get mad props from both of us.

The reality, however, is that piracy has existed and likely always will because there are people who will toss ethics out the window if it means getting something for free. If you have a streamlined process (e.g., DMCA takedown notice) in place for dealing with pirates, great. Use it. But don't let fighting piracy consume you. Don't let it take up all your time, especially when you should be writing.

A Drama Queen Troll will take this all-consuming need to defeat pirates to their support groups, meaning your time and energy are now focused on talking the troll down off the ledge or commiserating with them or explaining challenges or ... anything but writing. The focus doesn't have to be exclusively on piracy. It could be the latest scandal or a new development in the publishing industry (people usually react negatively to any change) or a misunderstanding about a change in the publishing industry that happened years ago.

That last one gives Nanette a headache, because there is one issue that seems to resurface every few months in her support groups as if it is the first time anyone ever talked about it. Most writers who rely on Amazon for any part of their publishing platforms are likely already aware that Amazon requires users of its platforms to spend $50 a year on Amazon before they can leave a review. This was a policy Amazon instituted as early as 2016 in an effort to combat the incentive for people to leave fake reviews (people were hiring review farms to flood Amazon with reviews of products they had never used). Whether you agree with the policy or not, whether it is effective or not, it has been around for several years at this point, yet every few months someone posts in a writing group how they are "outraged" by this "new" policy. In Nanette's experience, such posts have never been along the lines of "hey, I just learned of this, what do you think?" Instead they are posts filled with OUTRAGE (yes, caps are mandatory) and CALLS TO FIGHT IT. In other words, drama —drama that none of us have the time or energy for because we need to be writing.

Drama Queen Trolls are, for the most part, harmless in that they are having a highly emotional reaction to something we may or may not be able to control. However, there is a subset of Drama Queen Trolls that seem to go out of their way to produce an excessive amount of chaos and fear for the unsuspecting writer. In these cases, you can find yourself being sucked into the drama with that whole "deer in the headlights" look.

One example (and again, we're not going to share the author's name because we absolutely do not condone such behavior) is when a writer created a street team for his books. If you don't know what a street team is, it is basically a group of super-fans who like your work so much that they share your writings with others and engage in word-of-mouth campaigns (the most effective method of marketing) just because they like your work. Creative types gather these super-fans into groups (i.e., street teams) and often reward them with behind-the-scenes looks, advanced copies, and small gifts. In a healthy street team, the creative realizes that the super-fans are doing some incredibly powerful marketing that usually cannot be bought. Therefore, the creative shows gratitude to the members of the street team.

However, what happens when the creative makes certain demands on the street team? One writer did just that, and his demands were, ahem, excessive. He required that all members of his street team (1) buy his books, (2) review his books, and (3) promote his works via social media. Yes, you want your super-fans (and all fans) to buy your work and support you, but to demand that they do so is extreme. But this writer went further. Anyone who didn't meet his demands would be removed from his street team, and he expected them to do the work of proving that they were meeting his demands in a timely manner. When a member of his street team wrote to him privately to say this seemed too much of an ask for her, the level of rudeness escalated to insults and name-calling.

Imagine that you are a store owner and you require every person who enters your store to buy an item, tell others about how great that item is, and then tell others about your store so they can come follow the same process. How long do you think you would be in business?

So this writer was a troll for a whole lot of reasons, but he was not really being a Drama Queen Troll. However, he was feeding the Drama Queen Trolls all sorts of juicy morsels that they could then share with others. And they did. Repeatedly. One person who shared the post containing screen shots of the back-and-forth between the writer and fan generated more than two thousand comments.

Yes, as writers we need to be aware of such bad behavior by other "professionals" within the industry and, yes, we should have safe spaces where we can discuss these issues. The flip side is that these discussions can quickly spiral out of control and, before we know it, we are spending hours reviewing comments or even deleting comments when a viral post attracts trolls (and it will).

The Self-Aggrandizing Troll

Have you ever seen a post on social media by a fellow creative who is sharing a recent success or string of successes? Sharing what works for you with your colleagues is an excellent way of figuring out how to succeed and push yourself to achieve more, and such sharing posts can be inspiring for the novice creative and even the long-term pro who is just in a slump. Those motivating posts are awesome, and we love them.

But not all success posts are encouraging. In fact, Nanette tends to believe that most are passive aggressive attempts to say "look at me!" A helpful success post has at least two parts: a summary of the efforts made and the outcome. When the "efforts" are basically summarized as "I did the work and you can too," it's not really helpful. Those kinds of posts (i.e., "look at what I achieved, and I did it simply by doing the work as is generally considered the only "right" way to work) are the machinations of Self-Aggrandizing Trolls.

The problem with this trollish behavior is that it equates amount of work with success. If you do the work, you will succeed. Ergo, if you are not succeeding, it is because you are not doing the work. That reasoning can be disastrous to someone who actually is doing all the work and yet is not experiencing the same level of success as the troll.

Most twelve-step recovery programs have a saying something like if you work the steps, the steps work. But what happens if you don't know what the steps are? How can you work them to achieve success? This is what the Self-Aggrandizing Trolls are doing: They're telling you to work the steps, but they're not defining the steps.

Nanette and Jules are members of several of the same author support groups. In one such group, a regular contributor routinely posts about her successes, and she gives quite a bit of detail ... about the *achievement*. When people ask how she got there, her comments are always some variation of "I did the work" (meaning, in this instance, she wrote the books). Commenters often *ooh* and *ahh* over her posts, responding that they hope to be where she is one day. The problem is, she's not really sharing the full story.

Yes, she wrote the books, but she also invested five figures in advertising them (as she detailed in a different post) and got her books listed in the newsletters of some very big influencers in the genre.

If you're reading her success post and looking at the fact that she has written three books and is earning five figures a month from those three books, then comparing her numbers with your own ten books that you have published, from which you are earning $13 a month, you have just been trolled. The next step you take will likely lead you down the rabbit hole of imposter syndrome (which we'll discuss in the next chapter). Basically, you start to feel like a failure. You've "done the work" but you're not getting the same results, so maybe you're not meant to be a writer ...

NO! Stop that line of thinking right now. Like we said, those Self-Aggrandizing Trolls aren't sharing because they want you to succeed too (no matter how many times they claim that in their message). They are sharing because they want pats on the back and their own arms are too tired from all the self-patting. So the next time you read such posts, make sure you do so with a critical eye. When that troll says "do the work," do they define specifically what they did? If not, congratulate them and move on. If they did define it, make sure you understand how it differs from your challenges. A writer of journal articles will have a very different path to success than a writer of romance stories, who will have a very different path to success than a writer of horror novels. Glean what you can from people sharing their successes, but remember that sometimes people just want to gloat.

The Family Member Troll

So far we've been talking about friends and colleagues (whether you know them personally or not) who can demonstrate troll-like behavior that takes you away from your own writing. Now we're going to talk about family members—and we realize this can be a sensitive area for many readers, so please understand that we are by no means dictating how much or how little time you should spend with your family. Only you can decide that.

In fact, before going any further, take a moment to think about how you delineate your writing career from your family obligations. When is it appropriate for your family to interrupt your work? Will you answer your children's calls when they've already texted twice to say that it isn't important? Do you want your significant other to ask you a question as soon as they get the chance? Do you want your extended family to drop in whenever they're in the neighborhood, even if it means interrupting your only writing time? There are no right and wrong answers to these questions. All we're asking is for you to take a moment and define some boundaries for yourself and your family. Dr. Andrea Brandt explains that boundaries are important for many reasons, including creating physical and emotional safety, protecting your self-worth and ego, and reducing stress, conflicts, and misunderstandings. Once you have an idea of your expectations and desires, you are in a better position to identify troll-like behavior that creates a time and energy suck in your writing.

Okay, so now let's look at some examples of how family members can interfere with our writing careers.

One of the most obvious problems is when you are interrupted while you are "in the zone." Having a dedicated office area with a door to close you off from distractions is ideal, but life rarely affords us the ideal. Sometimes distractions simply cannot be avoided. For Nanette, one of her furries will inevitably get sick (or bark at an errant leaf on a tree or demand to go potty RIGHT NOW) right when she is in the thick of a highly productive writing streak. Meanwhile, Jules has to deal with interruptions by way of phone calls (more often than not, from Nanette). If you define your boundaries for yourself and your family members, the number of interruptions should decline and any interruptions that continue should fall more in the "yes, interrupt me" category (meaning they warrant an interruption because of an emergency nature or something that you want to be apprised of immediately, as opposed to an issue that can wait until you're done with work).

The more nefarious type of interruption comes from family members (and close friends) who don't have a clear understanding that your work is still work even if it doesn't take place in an office or more traditional office setting. They think you sit at home in your favorite jammies or occasionally head to the local coffee shop (especially on shower days), type up a few pages that takes maybe five minutes at most (because they know how long it takes to type up a few pages of email messages, and writing is nothing more than typing words on the page), and then spend the rest of your day sleeping or watching movies or puttering around the house. (They probably also think you make several thousand dollars a day off each of your books and that they could be successful as a writer because they have a bunch of great plot ideas, which they are willing to share with you for half the profit.)

When people don't understand the realities of what a writing career requires, they can unknowingly and unintentionally exhibit troll-like behaviors in the form of interrupting your workday. Such interruptions happen in numerous ways. For example, a cousin might call you up and ask you to provide emergency childcare for their eight- and ten-year-old because it's a day off at school and the cousin forgot. Sure the kids are mature enough that they shouldn't need your non-stop attention, but having them in the house will be a disruption to your work. Maybe you agree the first time. It is family, after all, right? But what about the second time? What about when that cousin calls and asks you to pick up the kids from school on an early dismissal day—twenty minutes from now?

What do you do when a friend you haven't spoken to for a few months calls out of the blue—right when you've hit the greatest writing streak of the month? Do you answer the phone, especially when you know this friend has a habit of talking for hours at a time? Then again, you haven't heard from them in months, and if you don't take the call, you might offend them or might not hear from them again.

How about when your significant other comes home from work or perhaps has a day off when you are on deadline: How much does their behavior distract you? They might interrupt you just to ask a quick question—perhaps even something about whether their watching TV in the other room will interrupt your work or if you would like them to go grab something for lunch so you can keep working ... But the interruption is still an interruption.

Edward Brown wrote an article detailing "The Hidden Costs of Interruptions at Work." He cited research that workers routinely lose 40% to 60% of their most productive time to "quick" interruptions (think "Got a minute?" questions). For a self-employed writer, losing half your productivity on a regular basis can be a death knell. Interruptions go beyond the initial interruption itself. Even after you are able to get back to writing, you now have to "restart" the process (and starting the process can be difficult for many people). You also have to recover the momentum that you lost. More insidious, you can unknowingly become frustrated by having to restart and rebuild, which can cause your enthusiasm for the writing to erode.

All because someone asked, "Got a minute?"

Brown concluded that the reason people allow these interruptions to occur is because they don't realize just how costly they are to productivity. We would argue that this is true of all troll-like behaviors, whether intentionally or unintentionally trollish, whether perpetuated by strangers, colleagues, friends, or family. Hopefully, now that you're learning about the different kinds of troll behaviors, you will be better able to spot the time and energy sucks affecting your most productive hours.

Again, we can't tell you what is right or wrong for your personal situation. All we can do is help you see when troll-like behaviors are impeding your work. How you choose to deal with them, if you do, is up to you, and we will offer some suggestions later. But before we do, we have one more troll to unmask.

Action Step #3

Continue filling in your chart to identify trolls that

may be in your work zone. Look at the actions/words of your professional associations, friends, and family, both online and in person. Continue tracking these activities until you start to see some patterns—whether in the trolls' activities or your own reactions to them. The goal is for you to have a better understanding of just how much these trolls are costing you (in terms of your productivity).

4-THE TROLL IN THE MIRROR

Now we come to a chapter than may be uncomfortable for some to read. The truth of the matter is that not all trolls are external. Some trolls are closer than we think. Some of us are trolls ourselves.

Yes, you might be a troll. You might even be your own troll.

When you were reading some of the earlier examples of troll behavior, did you feel indignant, as if we were calling you out personally for trying to share what you have learned with others so that they may avoid similar fates? Or did you race to Google some of the unnamed trolls we mentioned so you could then share their troll behaviors with your own group of friends and supporters?

Look, we get it. Sometimes you want to share your successes or the crazy drama exploding elsewhere online. We do too. That's how we know about most of the examples we've mentioned, whether specifically or in general descriptions—because we shared them with each other. So when we're talking about the Troll in the Mirror, we're not really focusing on that kind of troll behavior (although we do hope that after reading how trolls, whether intentional or not, affect others' productivity, whether they realize it or not, you might put some more thought into what you share and when).

But that's not really what we're talking about here. The Troll in the Mirror is when you engage in certain behaviors that adversely affect your productivity. Such behaviors can be as little as turning on the radio or TV for background noise when you work (some people need it, others can't stand it—to each their own) or as big as jumping head first into imposter syndrome.

The Troll in the Mirror is especially perilous because that troll knows far too much about how to invade your productivity in ways that will have you spiraling downward until, before you know it, it's been six months and the only writing you've done is to respond to emails.

This troll can affect you in three important and dangerous ways: create distractions, cause you to forego self-care, and send you on a trip to imposter syndrome land.

Creating Distractions

Let's go back to the background noise question. Again, some people swear by it, others can't tolerate noise at all. Nanette falls in the former group. She has to have background noise (in the form of TV or coffee shops) when she is performing certain work-related tasks. However, when doing other tasks, she absolutely cannot have the noise. For her, the Troll in Mirror does a fantastic job of convincing her otherwise:

> *Remember how productive you were yesterday? You were more productive than you've been in a long time! But everything was the same, right? Oh, wait. That's not entirely true. That's right, you had the TV on. Some reality show. Do you remember who won? No, of course not, because you were in the zone. You can do that again today, replicate that productivity. All you need to do is turn on the TV ...*

And twelve hours later she still has not gotten a single item on her to-do list marked off. These trolls are real, and they're powerful. They know just which buttons to push to convince you that what you absolutely should not be doing is actually exactly what you should be doing. What's more, when you start to realize that maybe you shouldn't have listened to that little voice in your head—after all, you have no work to show for the day—that voice will come back and convince you that the reason you didn't produce any words today is because you just weren't inspired. And you'll believe it. You'll lament about the loss of your muse and your inability to write as a result. (But of course, if you've read *Don't Scare Your Fairy*, you know that your muse doesn't really abandon you as long as you don't abandon her.)

Foregoing Self-Care

Another way that the Troll in the Mirror can sabotage your productivity is by causing you to ignore your self-care.

Okay, just to clarify, by self-care, we're not necessarily talking about washing your face, brushing your teeth, and brushing your hair, although we do highly recommend that you brush your teeth as recommended by your dentist. After all, we want to see those "Yes, I did it!" smiles in the author photo on your book jacket and/or media portfolios.

Self-care here means taking the steps necessary to ensure that you are continually rejuvenating yourself so that you always have a well of inspiration from which to draw. How you carry out such self-care is unique to you, but some general guidelines to follow include taking regular breaks, engaging in physical activity appropriate for your body, and celebrating your successes at all levels, no matter how big or small.

Taking regular breaks is an important step that

many people forget to do because what they define as a break is checking in on social media. If your work requires you sitting at a computer to be productive, then when you take your breaks periodically throughout the day, do not sit in the same position and continue doing the same kinds of repetitive tasks. Get up and move away from the computer. Stretch your hands, wrists, and arms, and move them around as much as possible. Stare out a window, focusing on the horizon. Take the dog for a walk and let your mind wander in whatever direction it chooses.

When you take a break, escape the computer. Your hands will thank you, your eyes will thank you, your legs will thank you, and your brain will thank you. Plus, as an added benefit, you will not get side-tracked by any troll behaviors that you unexpectedly run across online. It's a win–win situation.

Another aspect of self-care is to avoid sacrificing your breaks to help others. Remember that cousin who needs you to fill in as a childcare provider? Yeah, they're calling again—this time to run a quick errand for them because their car is in the shop. Perhaps you agree to help out during your scheduled break as this offers a good compromise (according to that little troll voice in your head). But is it really a good compromise? You are effectively agreeing to give up your self-rejuvenation time in exchange for having to go out in public (and if today isn't a shower day, you might need to get creative to make yourself presentable), endure traffic and parking challenges, deal with other people (who may or may not be having a good day), and then race back to your computer so you can jump back into your writing.

Except when you get back to your computer, your brain has been so engaged in the errand that it hasn't had time to replenish your creativity well. Gripping the steering wheel didn't allow you the opportunity to stretch your wrists, and now your hands are cramping when you try to type. Plus, you were in such a hurry to keep your momentum going that you forgot a bathroom break and didn't grab a snack, so now your body is sending you a million different signals to STOP WORKING NOW.

Your writing is a career, whether you are working part time or full time. Treat it as such, and you will be better able to ward off the trolls that are trying to steal your productivity. Regular breaks are a healthy part of any writing career, and when you see them as another task in your work day—a task that replenishes you, mind, body, and soul—you can reap the benefits by maintaining high levels of productivity throughout the day. Don't let that little troll voice in your head convince you otherwise.

Visiting Imposter Syndrome Land

The Troll in the Mirror wants you to believe that a visit to Imposter Syndrome Land is a one-way trip. It absolutely is not. While reading this section, if you find yourself thinking you can't escape imposter syndrome, come back here and re-read this:

You can escape Imposter Syndrome Land whenever you want. The choice is yours.

Melody Wilding describes imposter syndrome as follows:

> [Imposter syndrome] reflects a belief that you're an inadequate and incompetent failure despite evidence that indicates you're skilled and quite successful.

There are many ways that imposter syndrome can rear its ugly head, but when it comes to the writing community, the Troll in the Mirror usually steps up with an argument that goes something like this:

> *Look at that writer's work. They've been writing less than you have, and so many typos in their work. Ugh, and the writing itself is so ... boring. Trite. Been there, done that. You write so much better, right? But then how come they're doing so much better? They have way more followers than you, and they're making more money from their writing than you. They make more in one month than you did all*

*year. How is that possible? Maybe you're not writing enough. Maybe you're writing isn't as good as you think it is. Maybe your editor or agent is lying to you because they just want your money. Maybe you're not spending enough time writing. Maybe your ideas are too "out there." Maybe they're not "out there" enough. That's a lot of maybes. I'm not really sure what's going on, but it seems pretty clear to me that you're not a **real** writer ...*

At some point in our writing careers, the Troll in the Mirror will try to convince you that you are doing it wrong, not doing enough, doing too much—whatever extreme the troll offers, the outcome is the same: You question whether you are a real writer.

It doesn't help when you are being exposed to people like the Self-Aggrandizing Troll or even the Drama Queen Troll. Remember the writer who demanded that his street team support him monetarily and with free marketing? He's still got several books in the top ranks at Amazon, and he's consistently pulling in enough each month to work exclusively as a writer. If you did that to your readers, how many would stick around? Does it make you less of a writer if you answered zero? No, it doesn't, because you are a writer. Period. (By the way, if you're looking for tips, hints, and ideas for genuinely connecting with your readers, check out *Don't Stone Your Gnome*.)

When the Self-Aggrandizing Troll is sharing how they made ten thousand dollars in a single month from three short books, do you look at your catalogue of twenty-plus books and last month's earnings that barely made it into triple digits? Because that's exactly what the Troll in the Mirror wants you to do. It wants you to compare yourself to others and find yourself lacking—whether it is in the revenues generated, books/articles written, ads generated, blog posts published, or number of new fans signing up for your newsletter. It could even point to the number of hours you spend writing compared to other writers. As we said, this troll is the most dangerous of all because it knows your weaknesses and your fears and it maximizes the impact of its troll behaviors by zeroing in on those areas that will do the most harm.

Action Step #4

Continue filling in your chart to identify trolls that may be in your work zone. Look at your own actions/words/thoughts, both online and in private. Look for particular areas where the Troll in the Mirror seems to zero in on. How are you reacting to them? Which types of reactions have the best outcomes in terms of enabling you to continue being productive?

5-THE TROLL'S DEEPEST DESIRES

Even after reading all the descriptions of the different kinds of trolls, when you encounter one, many people instinctually want to fight back, especially with dealing with the All-Too-Familiar Troll. When facing other types of trolls, such as family members or the Troll in the Mirror, you might want to ignore or avoid them. Before you give in to your gut reaction, take a moment and think about what the troll in your sights wants.

Capture Your Soul

Okay, it might sound a bit melodramatic, but really, the troll wants to trap you in your inability to work by distracting you so much that you focus all your energy on them and forget about your own goals and dreams.

Trolls, especially online trolls, may be bored in real life and are looking for stimulation in a forum that makes it all too easy to create drama and get people talking about their antics. When you see a troll commenting on one of your posts or a friend's posts, the one thing you can do to make that troll's day is engage, either by reacting to them directly or sharing their comments with others.

Engagement is the online troll's drug of choice. Don't become their dealer, because they're demanding and apparently never sleep. They want all of your attention, every last bit of it. And if you're spending all your energy constantly putting out fires that the troll creates—whether online or by interrupting you or causing you to doubt yourself—you will have no energy to create.

If you can't create, the troll has succeeded in capturing your soul.

Diminish Your Excitement

Trolls are masters at siphoning off your time and energy in various ways, as we've already discussed. But even when you have your clearest troll-identifying goggles on and can escape their swipes at your coveted writing time, they may still be able to diminish your excitement for your writing, thereby impeding your progress and success.

Let's talk about a couple of examples to show how trolls can affect you even when you are doing everything right.

You've thought about your writing time and space, defined specific boundaries, and have informed your family and close friends about these boundaries so that they know when it is appropriate to interrupt your work. For the most part, everyone is on board because they want you to succeed too. But you have one friend who always calls five minutes before your scheduled breaks or right after you get back from lunch and are digging into the next big push. It's not in the middle of your writing time, so that's an improvement, but the calls still interrupt your flow at times (not all the time, though, if you're being honest).

There are two ways that this scenario diminishes your excitement. First, you're considering the need for a reminder to this friend that they need to respect your boundaries. For some people, this is not a problem. For others, even the thought of a possible confrontation can trigger anxiety-like reactions. In addition, if this friend calls fairly routinely, as you approach each break in your writing schedule, you might start glancing at the phone, wondering if they will call today. You become distracted from your writing and may even start to associate the negative feelings you are experiencing from the friend situation with your current writing project.

Another problem that arises is that, when your friend does interrupt your work flow, you must then restart the writing process. Starting can be a big obstacle for many writers, and now you have to start twice: once before your friend interrupted you and once again after your friend has moved on. But let's say that you pick up right where you left off with no problems. Your momentum has been interrupted, and it takes a while to ramp back up to your previous levels. You might feel frustrated by the need to rebuild your pathways for getting back in the zone where you were, which can lead to a loss of enthusiasm that permeates your work for the rest of your day.

The interruption can also lead to missteps and errors when you finally are able to get back on track. You may be so determined to get back into the flow of your writing that you completely forget the game-changing idea you had right before your friend called. Maybe you don't remember it for two or three hours, at which point you realize that the last few hours of writing no longer apply to your current project. The realization can completely drain you of all enthusiasm to keep writing that day.

The Troll in the Mirror will use these situations of waning enthusiasm to swoop in and tell you that you're an imposter, thereby compounding the issue. Being aware of how even less-than-fully-successful trolls can have an impact can help you take steps to prevent them from draining your enthusiasm.

Make You Miserable

Many of the types of trolls we've discussed in this book thrive on making people miserable. It's a sad commentary on humanity, but unfortunately true. The

Self-Aggrandizing Troll might be sharing incomplete pictures of their success (or even inflating their success in some way) because it's their way of making themselves feel better than someone else. It becomes an "us vs. them" mentality, where the "us" are the people who have succeeded in some fashion while the "them" have yet to replicate those same successes. Sure, some people genuinely want to share what is working for them in order to help others. Unfortunately, others are sharing because they want to be part of the "cool crowd" and the only way they can enjoy that category is if they are publicly recognized as having achieved that status.

But by propping themselves up, they are also tearing others down. They are pointing out that others haven't had this kind of success, which is what really matters. They are suggesting that you haven't really been doing all the work (even if you have been writing twenty-five thousand words a week) because you aren't on the pedestal with them. They are highlighting that they are up here while you are down there. They were once where you were, but now they have escaped.

Escaped. Ouch. Is your current situation something you need to escape?

Oh, look out ... here comes the Troll in the Mirror, swooping in to take you from questioning what you are doing wrong to full-blown imposter syndrome. Welcome to the world of the miserable writer.

When you approach potential trolls with a more critical eye, you are in a better position to understand why their seemingly harmless behavior can have such devasting effects on you. In addition, you can see how the network of trolls to which you are routinely exposed work together to steal your time and energy so you have nothing left for your writing.

Now that you have a better sense of the kinds of trolls lurking in around the corner, you can start developing a plan for dealing with them. We will talk about tricks and tips for dealing with trolls in the next chapter.

Action Step #5

Develop a policy for dealing with trolls. You will continue this in the next chapter, so for now, start with the big picture by defining your boundaries for your writing sanctuary. Don't worry about making them perfect to start; you'll tweak them as you see what works and what doesn't. These are just for you right now. As you are thinking about your boundaries, review the tracking chart to identify the kinds of trolls you tend to encounter on a regular basis. How can your writing sanctuary boundaries keep these trolls out? Remember that boundaries can be defined for others as well as yourself.

6-TROLL-PROOFING YOUR WRITING SANCTUARY

Whether you are writing in a home office with a door or the local coffee shop, you can use various tools and tips to make it harder for trolls to sap your time and energy.

Establish an Office Hours Policy

An initial step for creating a troll-free zone is to establish your office hours and what types of behaviors are appropriate during this time. Note that the office hours policy is for you as well as others.

You don't have to have an actual office to have office hours, and your office hours do not have to be a set schedule. If you like having defined times that dictate when you write, by all means, design a writing schedule. If you are more of a go-with-the-flow kind of writer or are dealing with competing schedules that are constantly changing (e.g., kids' school activities), you might define your office hours as "whenever I am sitting at the kitchen counter and my laptop is open." Make the policy work for you, defining as much or as little as you need to, but create some sort of boundaries.

The next step in your office hours policy is defining what activities are allowed and which ones are not while you are within your boundaries. Right now, we are talking about activities that you participate in. You can delineate specific times, such as saying that you will be writing from 2:00 to 4:00 and taking a ten-minute break to walk around the block at the top of each hour, or you might prefer to set word goals, saying you will write one thousand words and then do fifteen jumping jacks. Remember to indicate what you cannot do during this time as well. For example, you might decide that you cannot go online during your office hours. If you have to research something for a piece you are working on, that will have to wait until you have finished your office hours. Make a note to follow up on it later, then continue focusing on the present. We talk more about using schedules and policies to treat yourself well and keep your inner fire burning in *Don't Smother Your Dragon*.

Finally, define policies for how you want others to interact with you (or not) during your office hours. Perhaps you want your kids to call you at specific times if they have a question, or maybe you ask them to text instead of calling so you can respond during a break. You might ask your significant other to email you any reminders, while also explaining that you will not be logging on to the internet during your writing periods. Give your friends and family a heads up that you will be ignoring emails and text messages or turning your cell to vibrate only during work hours, but also tell them the best way to contact you in the case of an emergency (and yes, you likely have some friends and family who will need a little explanation on what specifically constitutes an emergency). You might have to get a bit creative with this, but it helps everyone understand that you are working and are unavailable for drama or errands. Nanette still has a landline. She doesn't give the number out to anyone except her closest family members. If there's an emergency, they know to call that number. Thankfully, the phone has never rung.

Ignore, Ignore, Ignore

Before we discuss specific tools for dealing with trolls, we have to single out the All-Too-Familiar Trolls (and you know they just love being in the spotlight!). These trolls are basically online bullies or people who like generating chaos just because they can. A quick online search for "how to deal with trolls" will return a lot of articles detailing different approaches you can take. The top approach in all of these articles is ignore

—and we agree that this is the best action you can take.

Ignore, ignore, ignore.

If you see an All-Too-Familiar Troll on social media, whether in a professional group or commenting on someone's post, walk away. Shut down your web browser. Watch a YouTube video about talking pets. Anything you need to do to ignore the troll.

These specific trolls feed on chaos and thrive in the spotlight. Don't give it to them. Some of the articles on dealing with trolls suggest you can also engage them by countering with facts, correcting mistakes, digging deeper into their psyche to figure out what's really bothering them, or even trolling them in return. However, we do not recommend adopting any of these approaches unless you happen to be a professional troll slayer or a psychiatrist with an inordinate amount of free time on your hands.

You might hear about someone who beat the trolls at their own game. Bravo to them! What you didn't hear is the hundreds or even thousands of people the troll bested first before finding someone who was better at trolling. Don't waste your time.

If you think you can best a troll, then why waste that energy on social media? Put it into your stories or write an article about beating trolls at their own games. If you want to really hurt the troll where it counts, succeed despite their best efforts because that means you're getting the spotlight, not them.

When You Can't Ignore the Trolls

There are times when ignoring the trolls is not really an option. When the trolls are coming to your website, are commenting on your posts and articles, or are trolling your fans on your social media pages, you need to take action to eradicate the problem as soon as possible.

Before you do anything, we have to say this again: Don't engage. It's not worth it.

Rather, what you should do is create an environment where troll behaviors are not tolerated. Whenever you are responsible for a platform where people come together as a community, whether it is your website/blog (where people can comment), on your social media pages, or in semi-private or private forums, you should always have a policy in place detailing what kinds of comments are appropriate and what kinds of comments/behaviors will be deleted and/or lead to users being blocked. You can also ask your fans and visitors to notify you if they see anyone infringing on your policy. Make your policy available to all visitors (e.g., a pinned post in a Facebook group), and periodically remind people that the policy exists, especially if you see a rash of troll behaviors. Mother Jones offers a fairly comprehensive example of such a policy.

. . .

Tip: Visit the websites/groups you use often and look for their commenting policies. If you can't find them, ask the owners/moderators. Reading what others have already put together can help you identify potential problem areas before they ever become a problem for you.

Once you have the policy in place, you are responsible for applying it. Having a policy and then allowing everyone to ignore it does no good for anyone. It creates an opportunity for breaking the rules, which the trolls love, and leads to more work for you as you sift through the wreckage. Remember, we're trying to eliminate time and energy sucks so you can focus on your writing.

You should include in your policy the repercussions of any inappropriate actions. You might offer a two-strikes system, meaning everyone is given a chance to make a mistake before they pay the consequences. Or you might inflict the consequences from the get go. There might be a mix of these as well, where certain actions are dealt with on a two-strikes system whereas others result in the harshest punishments immediately. For example, maybe one of your fans likes to share links to books that they wrote because they are trying to find readers. Such behavior might warrant a warning, asking the person not to self-promote; their original post is deleted, but if they do it again, they will be blocked. Meanwhile, another fan suddenly goes on a tirade, verbally attacking other commenters and even threatening them in some way. This could be a case when you delete the user from your group and/or block them from your page.

Most social media platforms have some form of block/ban so you do not have to even allow the trolls into your playground. Do not be afraid to use these if the situation warrants it, and it is better to ban/block early rather than let the trolls do their dirty work and then block or ban them.

If you have a street team or a circle of trusted fans, you can ask them to help out on your social media pages by moderating your pages and groups for you. A word of caution: making someone a moderator gives them more permissions on social media than the general user. Before you give anyone moderating permissions, make sure you have done your due diligence to the best of your abilities. Look at that person's commenting behavior in other areas outside of your group, if possible. If you mainly interact on Facebook, go read their tweets on Twitter or read their reviews on Goodreads (just don't read reviews of your own works on Goodreads [this reminder brought to you by Jules]). Also, before you give anyone moderating permissions, have a plan in place for removing those permissions if things don't go as plan. When you know how you will act before you have to, it makes the entire process much easier. Never give anyone access to areas that include financial information unless you have run a thorough background check on the individual.

When you are dealing with a Google It Troll, a Drama Queen Troll, or a Self-Aggrandizing Troll within one of your professional communities, you might want to consider "hiding" that person from your feed. When you block/ban someone, they cannot access your social media account on that platform. It's as if you don't exist. When you hide that person from your feed, you are still connected to them in some way (whether directly or via group membership) and they can see your public activity, but your feed will not be clogged with their trollish behaviors, which can make social media a more pleasant experience. Facebook has instituted a feature that enables you to hide (Facebook calls it "snooze") other users from your feed for thirty days. You will not see their posts or their comments on any posts during this time.

Most, if not all, social media platforms and other public commenting forums offer a way to report users that break the platforms' terms of service, which can include trolling. For example, one writer friend published a book on Amazon under a pen name. A particularly nasty troll figured out it was her and published a scathing review of the book on Amazon, except the review had nothing to do with the book itself. Rather, the review went on and on about what a horrible person the author was. Sadly, this is not against Amazon's terms of service. However, the troll then included the author's home address in the review, which is explicitly against Amazon's terms of service. We used the report function on the review to bring it to Amazon's attention, and the address information was redacted.

Again, don't be afraid to use the report function if you see trollish behavior happening in groups, on feeds, or even on blogs and other websites. If you can detail specifically how the troll is breaking the website's or group's policies, do so. Providing a little context can help the human reviewer on the other end see where the trolls really are.

Write/Talk It Out

Sometimes we just can't escape the trolls. They are everywhere, and no matter what we do, we can't stop ourselves from reacting to them. It's human nature to react to the stimuli around us.

When you find yourself suddenly itching to take a troll down a notch or two, ask yourself one question: If I react to this troll in a public space or private forum, what will the ultimate outcome be?

You cannot change a troll. You cannot make a troll stop being a troll. And even if you could, it would likely be a short-term change at best, and wouldn't you rather be spending your time and energy on writing?

When you feel attacked or sidetracked by a troll, take a step back and ask yourself if engaging the troll will really make a difference in how you feel. Remember, trolls have an uncanny way of invoking the Troll in the Mirror, and it is very possible that your initial reaction to some online troll is simply the Troll in the Mirror paving the way to Imposter Syndrome Land. Don't give them the power to control you.

Instead of engaging the troll directly, write or talk out your frustrations and reactions. If you think you may have some troll slayer in your genes, maybe you can write a scene in which a troll gets trolled. Perhaps you can write a satirical essay on the explosion of the troll population in the twenty-first century. If you want to vent about trolls in general, write it all out or talk to a trusted friend who understands the difficulties that trolls bring.

Whether you decide to write out your reactions or talk to a friend about them, do so in a private space. Never vent in a public forum or any area where you cannot control the narrative, such as a chat room or discussion group. Discussing trolls in public spaces has the potential to bring unnecessary drama to other users of that public forum, potentially distracting them from their writing if they have a strong reaction to your own experiences. In other words, don't become a

Drama Queen Troll. Furthermore, no matter how non-descript you may be during your chatting, you could provide enough clues that others will know which troll you are talking about. This can create a few problems. That troll might have friends in the group, and those friends might go tell the troll that you're talking poorly about them. The friends might gang up on you and make the trolling exponentially worse. Alternatively, other group members might interpret your venting as a call to action and then go attack the person who they think is being the troll (whether they are correct or not). A third possibility is that the other group members shame you for not having a thick enough skin or not protecting yourself before the troll ever showed up.

Again, before you do anything, ask what the possible outcomes could be. You can only control your own actions and reactions. Once you put them into a public space, they will take on a life of their own. Instead, shift the perspective from the focus on your raw emotional reaction to a more objective approach. In this way, you shut the trolls down before they even know you're on to them.

Protect Yourself

No matter how careful you are, you might not be able to fend off a troll attack on your own. If you have an online presence, you are a target for trolls.

Most online platforms have a policy in place for

dealing with trolls. If a troll comes for a visit in your neck of the cyberspace, report them to the appropriate platform owners—and keep reporting them until action is taken. Sometimes it requires perseverance on your part.

If a troll ever makes a threat of physical violence, reveals private information about you, or posts compromising or intimate photos (genuine or faked), contact the authorities. This includes the owners of the platforms where the threats are made as well as the police. Although trolling is itself not a crime, many states have laws against harassment, stalking, and bullying. Take screen shots of everything and share the information with the authorities.

Action Step #6

Continue with your policy for dealing with trolls. Now that you have your office hours policy, look at the specific kinds of trolls that you are most likely to encounter. What specifically will you do when you see these trolls? Put your action steps in writing.

You should now be finalizing three sets of guidelines: one for fans and followers who comment on your social media sites and/or websites, one for friends and family in terms of your office hours, and one for what steps you will take when you encounter a troll. Publish your commenting policy so your fans and followers know your expectations; share your office hours policies with your friends and families for the same reason. Finally, keep your policy for dealing with trolls somewhere where it is easily accessible for you. Refer to it whenever you find someone sneaking in to steal away your time and energy. Tweak it as necessary, especially when you identify a new troll. (And if you do discover a new kind of troll, make sure to visit our Facebook group (www.facebook.com/HealthyWriting-Career) so you can warn others. The sneaky little buggers like to diversify.)

7-DON'T BE A TROLL

Having read about the different kinds of trolls, you might be second-guessing yourself and your online actions. Do you find yourself engaging in troll-like behavior? We're here to help.

Not everyone will agree with our definitions of trolls, and that's okay. Maybe while you were reading about the Self-Aggrandizing Troll, you disagreed with the idea that sharing success stories is a form a trolling. It's true. Simply stating that you were successful is not a trollish behavior. The trick is in the details.

Let's consider the following scenario: T. R. Oll is an up-and-coming author who published his first book two months ago and quickly followed up with books two and three. He then writes a blog post highlighting his successes so that other authors can learn from what he did. Perhaps he even mentions specific details that helped him succeed, such as "advertising in newsletters" and "guest posting on blogs."

Great!

After carefully reading his experiences and analyzing whether the same kinds of tactics are appropriate for your writing, you decide to follow his guidelines. You spend the exact same amount of money advertising in newsletters and develop guest posts for the same number of blogs, although both the newsletters and blogs are appropriate for your genre (rather than using the same resources Mr. T. R. Oll did as he writes in a different genre). Unfortunately, even after following his detailed suggestions, your outcome is nowhere near his successes. Some may chalk this up to the finicky nature of the marketing world, but you decide to contact Mr. T. R. Oll privately to ask for any insights.

He replies, and you are excited as you open his email. Maybe now you can tweak your efforts ...

Except his email tells you point blank that the newsletters and blogs generated zero return on his investment. He also explains that he hired a PR firm and what he listed in his original blog post was what they told him they were doing for him.

Was he being vindictive or malicious in his original blog post? No. Did his incomplete information cause you to waste time, energy, and already limited marketing resources on something that he knew didn't work for him? Yes. Does that make him a troll? Probably not, but his blog does demonstrate troll-like behaviors, and that is what we have been focusing on.

We know that we can't control anyone's actions but our own, but if we can become more critical in how we interpret information (or a lack of information), we can avoid wasting our time and energy and instead focus on writing.

If you are concerned that maybe some of your blog posts, articles, or social media comments might be demonstrating troll-like behaviors, reach out to us either via email (info@healthywritingcareer.com) or in our Facebook group.

Action Step #7

Katy Preen offers a different approach to dealing with trolls by using it to enhance your writing skills. You can read about it in her Medium article "Feeding the Trolls."

8-SURVIVING IN A TROLL-FILLED WORLD

Trolls are becoming a fact of life. A YouGov survey from 2014 found that more than a quarter of Americans have made malicious comments online. That was five years ago, before trolling became as sophisticated in its attacks as it is today. Trolls will continue to branch out, looking for new ways to disrupt your life. Hopefully you are now better prepared to identify them and ignore them so you can focus on your writing career.

Remember that the most vicious of trolls are looking for ways to attack the unsuspecting person in random, unsolicited, and almost always public ways. However, as we have discussed in this book, when we consider trolls to be anything that takes our time and energy away from writing, we can find them in all sorts of cracks and crevices in our lives.

You can't change a troll, but you can manage your own actions/reactions as well as make your expectations known. Continue working on your commenting policy (for online activity), your office hours policy (to keep your writing time focused on writing), and your personal policy for dealing with trolls. Tweak each of these policies as necessary, and review them periodically to make sure that you are following the guidelines that you established.

Writing is ultimately a career. We embrace it because of the creative freedoms it affords us, but we shouldn't be sacrificing our productivity just because we enjoy expressing ourselves in words. Adopting a more business-like attitude toward our writing space and time can help ensure that we continue to have the writing space and time in which to thrive.

Just say no to trolls!

REFERENCES

Sources:

Elise Moreau, Internet Trolling: How do you spot a real troll? https://www.lifewire.com/what-is-internet-trolling-3485891

Dr. Andrea Brandt, Why Boundaries Are Important for a Healthy Relationship, https://thriveglobal.com/stories/why-boundaries-are-necessary-for-a-healthy-relationship/

Edward Brown, The Hidden Costs of Interruptions at Work, http://fastcompany.com/3044667/the-hidden-costs-of-interruptions-at-work

Melody Wilding, 5 Different Types of Imposter Syndrome (and 5 Ways to Battle Each One), http://themuse.com/advice/5-different-types-of-imposter-syndrome-and-5-ways-to-battle-each-one

YouGov, Over a quarter of Americans have made malicious online comments, https://today.yougov.com/topics/politics/articles-reports/2014/10/20/over-quarter-americans-admit-malicious-online-comm

ABOUT THE AUTHORS

Nanette M. Day

Dog wrangler, cat slave, turkey observer, cow racer, raccoon enabler...these are just a few of the jobs that keep Nanette busy on her acreage. When she's not watching Mother Nature's songbirds, quadrupeds, and creepy crawlies, Nanette writes books detailing their shenanigans. In addition to writing humorous vignettes of how her dog and cats are taking over the world (one nap at a time), she writes gritty flash fiction and short stories as well as small-town romance novels.

You can find Nanette at www.NanetteMDay.com

J.S. Dixon

Fuzzy sock collector, martini connoisseur, and dandelion enthusiast, author Jules Dixon writes contemporary M/F and LGBT romance, including the Triple R Series of seven New Adult romance titles, the M/M cowboy contemporary romance series Cherry County Cowboys, including *Spurs, Chaps,* and *Whips.* She also writes the popular multi-story series Holiday Hotties of short MM holiday-inspired stories as Rowan Nash. And now the Building a Healthy Writing Career and Productive Author non-fiction series. She loves tackling hard subjects with a little humor and a spark of sizzle.

You can find Jules at:

www.julesdixon.com

http://www.facebook.com/JulesDixonAuthor

https://twitter.com/JulesofTripleR

https://www.pinterest.com/JDixonAuthor

https://www.instagram.com/julesdixonauthor/
https://bookandmainbites.com/JulesDixonAuthor

Nanette M. Day

Puppy Kisses Book 1

**Mover and shaker. Squirrel chaser. Love muffin. Blanket
hog.**

For a dog in the country, it's important to run faster than the
bunnies through the acreage obstacle course, greeting the
turkeys and deer as they enjoy the breakfast buffet, chasing
down any pesky raccoons who think they own the place,

checking on the opossums to make sure they're not just "playing dead" (fool me once...), and serenading the neighborhood cows—all while keeping an eye on all those squirrels and their shenanigans.

Puppy Kisses is full of (mostly truthful) stories about the escapades of Pistachio, a dog on a mission to be everybody's friend (except maybe those pesky raccoons).

C. Jai Ferry

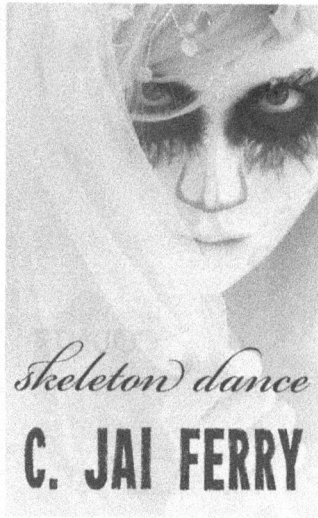

skeleton dance
C. JAI FERRY

Skeleton Dance

"My grandmother wanted to kill me..."

So begins a dark and disturbing look into a world that is all too real for thousands of children every day. "Skeleton

Dance" is the story of one young girl's perseverance in surviving the eccentricities of her grandmother. Despite being harassed in a multitude of ways, this young girl is able to stand up to her grandmother in both small and grandiose ways. Sometimes victorious, but more often not, she ultimately grows into a woman faced with the biggest challenge yet: Follow the well-worn path of the matriarchs in her family or strike out into virgin territory.

2014 winner of the Vermillion Literary Project Short Story Contest.

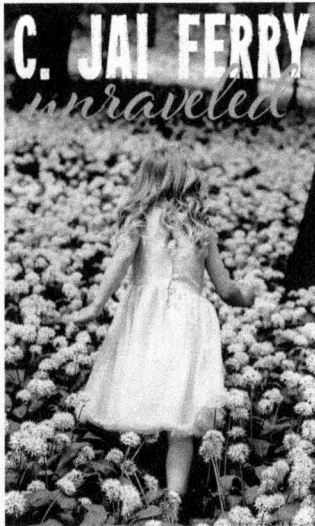

Unraveled: A collection of flash fiction and short stories

Step into a world of struggling fathers, aging English teachers, terrified mothers, plague-bearers, revenge artists, ill-fated lovers, and children searching for their place in life —all characters brought to life in the flash fiction of C. Jai Ferry. Ferry uses evocative language and imagery to highlight those telling moments when a person's entire life changes from a seemingly simple decision. These bite-sized morsels, most fewer than 100 words, examine the human condition and all its bittersweet moments.

J.S. Dixon

Essential Secrets for Building Successful Writing and
Critique Groups: Productive Author Series

https://www.amazon.com/J-S-Dixon/e/B07YGSTRBJ/

https://www.amazon.com/Jules-Dixon/e/B00PUSNF90/

https://www.amazon.com/Rowan-Nash/e/B07YF448MC/

A MONROE FALLS *romance*   2018 RITA® FINALIST

IN HIS ARMS

JULES DIXON

2018 RITA Finalist

In His Arms: A Monroe Falls Romance

Ten years ago Kiera Redfern left Monroe Falls and moved father and farther away. An invitation to the opening of a time capsule triggers the vague memory of her contribution and prompts her return. No one needs to see that letter, and definitely not Zach Lorton. When heated memories become fresh temptation, Kiera has to decide between changing the past or fighting for her future.

Zach never thought she'd be there, but after a night of revelations and a kiss that can't be ignored, he's ready to help Kiera heal from the past. When his boss demands his return to NYC, Zach has a choice to make—continue the abuse that's followed him through his childhood or stand up for himself and be the man he wants to be for Kiera.

Both will find out... is it better to be forgiven or forgotten?

In His Arms was originally part of the *Falling: Small Town Love Anthology.*

Triple R Series (A rainbow of love!)

Run to Love: Triple R 1

Personal trainer Jude Saylor's sense of direction in life has always been a little questionable. After a move and new job, he seems to be on the right path—until a cautious and sweet new client enters into the picture. Soon Jude wonders if happiness isn't as simple as a direction, but if it could be the woman he has next to him on the journey.

Presley Bradenhurst is a go-getter, as evidenced by her hundred pound weight loss, but the alteration to the outside didn't quite transfer to the inside. When Presley's trainer is fired and Jude steps up as the one who wants to make her sweat, will her instinct to run keep her from knowing a love she's only dreamed about?

In the end, can a lost soul and a broken soul work it out?

Rest, My Love: Triple R 2

~Editor's Pick~

Ex-soldier Rahl Vendetti returned to his hometown after watching three of his friends die. He should've died too. The guilt weighs on him and every breath is fed by a demon of war that taunts his future.

Singer and interior designer Sage Whiteman hit a genetic jackpot when it comes to dying young. She's living on borrowed time, so letting people in isn't easy, but the bartender with teddy bear eyes makes her wonder if it's time to open up.

They have plenty of chemistry between the sheets, but do they have the ability to be what the other needs outside of the bedroom, too? Sage may be the angel to bring out the gentle giant in Rahl, but can he be the strength she needs to face her uncertain future? Will they save each other and create something unexpected?

Ride With Love: Triple R 3

Motorcycle shop manager Kanyon Hills prides himself on being an honest and upstanding guy until a past one-night stand walks into his life and lets him know that he helped create the bubbling five-year-old, Grace.

Soon he's given a choice—his child or his girlfriend, Willow. His choice haunts him every day. Chef Willow Harper puts everyone's needs and happiness before her own. When Kanyon announces they are over, he creates a deep fissure in her heart, but her sixth sense tells her that a love like theirs will never truly be over and her heart will wait.

Can Willow learn to put herself first and find her own happiness with or without Kanyon? Will Kanyon grow from his past mistakes and return to the woman who fills his heart's crevices, or will he sacrifice his heart to the woman who had his child?

Road to Love: Triple R 4

Playboy Oliver Aston never hid who he is from anyone, and he finds it hard to understand when someone does just that. Betrothed at birth to the local town sweetheart, cowboy Holt Jamison spent his life believing that revealing his true self would disappoint his family, but after finding his heart's other half, that justification is getting harder and harder to stand by.

After a heated lovers quarrel in the desert, Oliver is sent back to the States alone and wondering if he's not one who's meant for love. When Holt leaves the military and moves far from his Alabama home to Oliver's hometown, is it a second chance the two hearts deserve? Or will a woman from the past come knocking to stake a claim on one of them?

Ready for Love: Triple R 5

Advertising account executive Jace Zelensky has a lover that won't ever have a heart beat.

Personal trainer and former soldier Kai Thomas worries that when it comes to love her heart may have been permanently broken at a young age.

When Jace's blind commitment to her job interferes with Kai's attempts to make a true connection and leaves Kai searching for her neurotic dog, Waffles, can Jace come to the rescue? Will a night with a no-strings-attached promise be the release they both need to satisfy their curiosity, or will those few minutes lead to something they're willing to risk their hearts for?

Ribbons of Love: Triple R 6

Avery Knicely grew up with three older brothers who can't see her as anything but the family's baby. What she really wants and needs is twisted with doubts, but after the ways of her brothers, she's positive she doesn't need a man to hover over her.

Security specialist Bryson Welch's controlling and manipulative twin sister reminds him on a daily basis why he joined the army and why he never should have returned home to endure the toxic relationships his sister and mother perpetuate. A blind date leads to a cold but eye-opening night in his vehicle and fulfills a Christmas wish for Bryson.

Will he be able to show Avery he can take care of her in the ways she really needs without overpowering her? Or will family come between the young lovers and lead Avery to question his true intentions?

Rescued by Love: Triple R 7

Aurora Jessen lives a life that would make a princess envious, but will her prince ever find her with her overprotective father hovering? When the infuriating Drexel Mason returns to town, his ability to get her to almost spontaneously orgasm while simultaneously making her want to stab him fascinates her, but a deadly accident reiterates the lack of control over her own life.

Drexel Mason's childhood was more a scene from a nightmare than a tale of fated love. The memories make him cover his pain with a secret elixir, but Aurora's kiss confiscates the lingering ache. When she accidentally takes his pain-killing potion, he's given an opportunity to slay the dragon of his cruel past and release the prince hiding inside.

Will Drexel save his princess or will she continue waiting for true love in her ivory tower?

Cherry County Cowboys Series

Spurs: Cherry County Cowboys 1

M/M Romance

Dr. Grayson Taylor is convinced that a summer fling with the bartending cowboy is a quick remedy to mend his broken heart. Soon his plans to return to big city lights for a dream career don't seem as attractive as the cowboy with dimples lying in his bed. When Grayson's charred past reappears, can he learn that forgiveness costs less than pride and admit he is the one who needs to be healed?

Cowboy Izaac Scott drove into town with little more than boots on his feet, a well-loved baseball cap on his head and a cross-country journey on his mind, but he's not sightseeing. He's running from the ghost of a first love. Will the doctor be the one to help Izaac realize that true love can heal the past or will the cruel spurs of life jab him in the heart again?

Chaps: Cherry County Cowboys 2

M/M romance

Rising rodeo star Nate O'Neill never expected to be living in a small Nebraska ranching town waiting for his rodeo brother to recover from a vicious ride. His unplanned stop steers him into the arms and bed of local celebrity, Tennessee Reed. Soon he questions what thrills him more —the rodeo or Tenn. Forced to face his reckless past, he's reminded that relationships can cause damage far worse than any bull ride ... and maybe he's headed for the same suffering again.

Professional football draft-pick Tennessee Reed returns home emotionally shattered by the unexpected passing of his father who left Tenn with a hereditary secret buried in his chest. He might be dying inside, but when Nate walks into his life all Tenn's troubles seem to disappear into those hazel eyes and he's never felt more alive. Will Tenn follow the cowboy wherever life leads? Or will he protect his heart and watch those fringed leather chaps ride away?

Whips: Cherry County Cowboys 3

Dune Wexley's unrelenting efforts to take down a local crook ended his law enforcement career and his father's life. Dune's lived in seclusion ever since. A Sunday drive to check on his mysteriously disappearing herd of cattle ends with a guest in his house, one who makes him reconsider isolating his shielded heart. But can this stranger be trusted?

Mason LaFleur answered an ad in the paper that held the promise of becoming a real cowboy on an authentic ranch, but that never happened. Instead Mason was forced to run away from a cruel man, but a miscalculation finds him bouncing off the hood of a truck and into the arms of a genuine cowboy.

When Mason is kidnapped, Dune must decide if getting revenge for his father's death is more important than saving the man who's offered up his heart and life to heal the broken cowboy.

Owned by the Alpha: Manlove Edition

M/M Romance

"Owned by the Alpha: manlove Edition is highly recommended!" —TBR Pile Reviews

NEW Dark Paranormal Romance Stories by International Bestselling Evernight Authors!

The Alpha lives for the hunt...

Driven by instinct, an Alpha shifter recognizes his fated mate from one scent, one touch. He'll pursue his man, regardless of the cost, and anyone else would be smart to get out of his way. He won't stop until he takes possession of his prize.

Although the hunter doesn't need convincing, his mate certainly does. The Alpha will have to prove himself as a lover and convince his man that he plays for keeps.

Includes stories: A Tiger's Luck by Maia Dylan, Last Alpha Standing by James Cox, **Mooncrest by Jules Dixon,** His Guardian Panther by Elena Kincaid, The Scarf by L.J. Longo, A Matter of Trust by Pelaam, Conflict of Interest by L.D. Blakeley

Checkered Flag Series

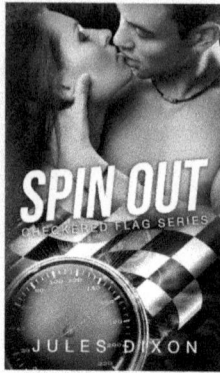

SPIN OUT: Checkered Flag Series 1

Reagan Breckle lost two things after leaving Linden College... eighty pounds and her crush on racing prodigy Thayr Westfield. Her passion for racing has brought her to the ISCaR Formula 1 racing competition where she has the chance to prove herself and beat Thayr at his own game. Even though she tries to fight them, the intense feelings she had for Thayr return. When her team's car is sabotaged and their sponsoring professor goes missing, Reagan's leadership is tested and her dream is jeopardized. How can she protect her heart, when she needs Thayr to save her dream?

Thayr Westfield is shocked he never noticed Reagan when she was on his team, but he's definitely noticing her now. His heart burns for her, but he questions if she'll let him in when he broke her trust a year ago? When his estranged birth father shows to the competition, and a dream internship goes awry, Reagan is the only part of his life that feels right. But when Reagan needs him, will Thayr be able to get past the deep hurt he suffered as a child and ask the one person who was never there for him to help the woman he loves?

Coming Soon!

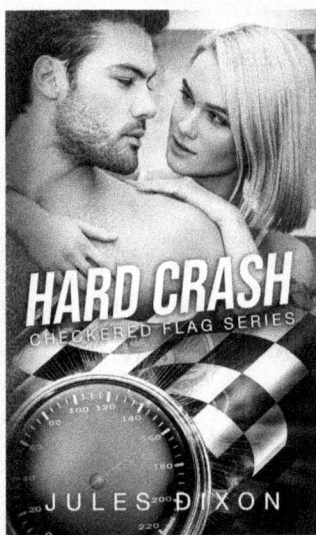

HARD CRASH: Checkered Flag Series 2

The story of Max Bowen and Savannah Monroe. They say rubbin' is racin' and these two put that saying to the test.

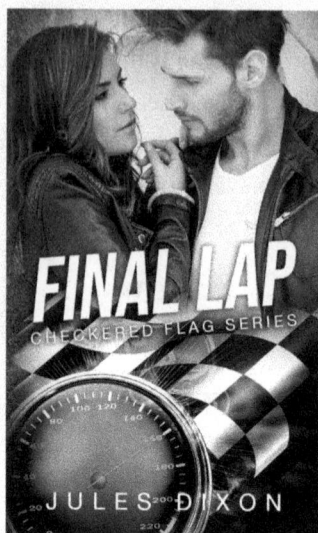

FINAL LAP: Checkered Flag Series 3

The story of Cameron Jones and Sophie Oestmann Find out what happens when two lovers race to the finish line.

Holiday Hotties by Rowan Nash

Winter Wishes

A sexy Santa, a matchmaking Aunt, and a wish he never thought would come true.

Sexy Santa was never on his list, but Caleb Gilden stopped writing a Christmas wish list long ago. Santa had always come up short in fulfilling his wishes. That's why he's put all of his money and time into his gift shop—at least others can get what's on their wish list.

Reeve Stone wishes for a different outcome of a day when his parents died in a horrific car crash right in front of him and his sister. He knows that isn't going to happen, so he'll just keep a smile on his face for his sister's sake.

But when Reeve meets the green-eyed gift shop owner and is forced into donning a Santa suit for a sick and disadvantaged children's holiday party, will he finally grant a wish for Caleb?

And will Caleb help Reeve through the hardest day of the year only to discover love is what they've both been wishing for?

Snowflake Smiles

A blizzard, a moody Christmas tree farmer, and a chance to be what each other needs.

Race car driver Ben Carver's trip home takes a detour when the storm of the decade dumps on his plans. With no available hotels, he's committed to riding out the storm and holiday in a restaurant until his phone buzzes and a stranger announces he's come to save Ben from a Christmas alone. Ben's ready for a new challenge in his fast-moving life, but the brooding tree farmer might have too many secrets that will keep them from getting their relationship to the checkered flag.

Christmas tree farmer Ford Lennox returned to western Nebraska after his parents passed away in quick succession and left unanswered questions about how he really came into the world. He dedicates himself to reviving his parent's business and giving holiday happiness to others, much to the detriment of his personal life, but one night snowed in with the comfort of the blazing fire and a man who makes his heart race might change his thinking. He's hidden too much for too long and maybe the past doesn't matter as much as the future does.

Will Ford end up being the best Christmas gift Ben's ever received? Find out now!

Frozen Faith

A dream on the line, a hockey date that's not to watch the game, and a man whose heart has been frozen by past relationships.

Dayne Swift didn't imagine the last-hope loan for his business would be accompanied with a flirty loan officer, but he'll take both. After coming out, Dayne's family told him don't come back and since then, he's kept to himself, only confiding in one other person—his ex-girlfriend from college—and she's cheering him onto the goal.

Burned one too many times by love, Will Howard knew the opportunity to invest in Dayne's business was the right call, and Will can't help but think the sweet and nervous furniture designer is worth taking a chance on, too. He asks Dayne to join him at a hockey game, but little does Dayne know he'll be on the ice and not in the stands.

When the loan's in jeopardy, can Dayne come up with a different plan for his business to save his future and can Will find the faith to believe Dayne is worth fighting for when he's frozen with memories of past choices?

Champagne Cheers

A failing business, a man with the means to save it, but in the end, they might find they both need to be saved.

Aspiring venture capitalist Matteo Bianci III has one chance to prove himself to his brutally honest father or his dreams of becoming a partner in the Bianci business will be over.

Sent to asses the return potential of several Niagra-on-theFalls area vineyards, Matteo's short business visit turns into an unplanned vacation when a lake-effect blizzard causes whiteout conditions and the airport closes. Matteo's attraction to the bed and breakfast and vineyard's owner isn't in his future plan, the solid plan he's had since his was fourteen. Falling can't happen, but still he wonders, what it would be like to have someone to kiss on New Year's Eve.

Janek Becker's vineyard is struggling, so when the stubborn rich guy shows at his door declaring he has a reservation in his closed bed and breakfast, Janek's torn between turning him away into the snow or making a pitch to the man who could save his future. When the vineyard's generator stops working and equipment breaks in the fermenting house threatening the year's wine, can they work together to save the crop?

Will Matteo realize a good endeavor when he sees one and invest his heart? Or will he decide that the Three Cheers Winery and Janek aren't worth the risk?

Other stories to come:

Puppy Presents

Two adorable puppies, two men with broken hearts, and the chance for all to have a happy new year.

This year Kiel Rushton wishes for something with a beating

heart and maybe a wagging tail. A trip to the local shelter finds him facing a tough decision when he discovers that two dogs, Mistletoe and Holly, are destined not to see the New Year. He's never had a fish, much less a dog. The kennel worker with twinkling eyes seems to think he could handle the responsibility, but responsibility has always been Kiel's middle name.

Brady Littleton works the shelter every Saturday, more reliable than even the postal delivery person. When it comes to a dog being the right fit for someone, his gut has never been wrong, but it's been wrong about a man being his right fit—way too many times. The timid soon-to-be dog owner just needs some encouragement and maybe a doggie play date with his own dog to show him the season is meant for caring.

Will Brady be able to convince Kiel the two dogs were meant to be in his life? Will Kiel convince Brady that he was meant to be there, too?

Jingle Bell Joy

Candy Cane Cupid